# *LIGHT*

## *SCIENCE SECRETS*

Jason Cooper

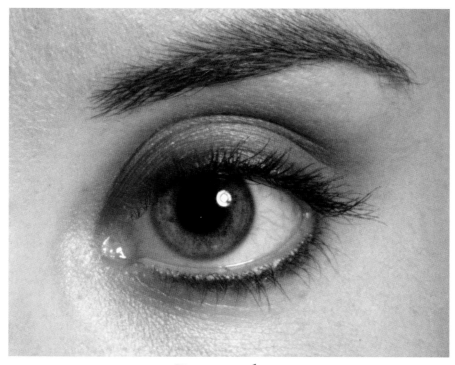

Rourke

Publishing LLC

Vero Beach, Florida 32964

www.rourkepublishing.com

PHOTO CREDITS: © Photodisc: Cover; © Painet, Inc.:title page, page 21; ©K-8 Images: page 4; © Lynn M. Stone: pages 8, 12, 13, 18; courtesy NASA, page 7, 17; © Archive Photo: page 10 ; courtesy Sharplan Lasers, Inc. , page 15

Title page: *The human eye needs light to see.*

Series Editor: Henry Rasof

Cover and interior design by Nicola Stratford

**Library of Congress Cataloging-in-Publication Data**

Cooper, Jason, 1942-
  Light / Jason Cooper.
     p. cm. — (Science secrets)
Summary: Provides a simple discussion of the sources and kinds of light, colors, and how eyes see.
Includes bibliographical references and index.
  ISBN 1-58952-411-X (hardcover)
  1. Light—Juvenile literature. [1. Light.] I. Title. II. Series:
Cooper, Jason, d 1942- Science secrets.
  QC360 .C66 2002
  535—dc21
                                        2002015711

Printed in the USA

# TABLE OF CONTENTS

## LIGHT AND DARK

Light lets most people see things. On a bright day we can easily see things all around us. When light disappears, we are in the dark.

Light is a form of **energy**. We get light from several places. We make some of our light. But most of our light comes from nature. It comes from the sun.

*Lights brighten city skylines.*

# LIGHT FROM THE SUN

The sun is a star and appears as a distant ball of light in the sky. The sun produces light and heat that travel 93 million miles (150 million kilometers) through space to reach us.

The sun's light makes daylight. It also makes the earth warm enough so that we can live in most places. Without the sun to warm us, the earth would be too cold a place to live.

*The sun: nature's heat and light*

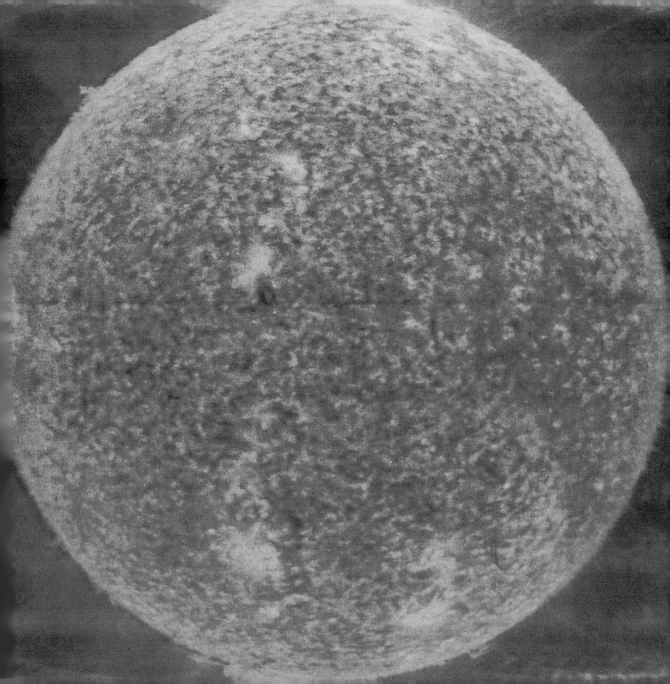

## SUNLIGHT AND PLANTS

Sunlight warms our air. It also lights our way so we can see things. And sunlight is also "food" for plants.

Most plants need sunlight to grow. These plants include flowers, vegetables, trees, and grass. Many animals depend on these plants for food sources.

*Plants need sunlight to grow.*

## MAN-MADE LIGHT

What do we do when there is no sun to let us see? We need to see at night, and we need to see in dark places. Early people lit open fires in caves and camps. This helped them to see in the dark.

As time went on, people needed better ways to see. In 1882 Thomas Alva Edison set up a power station in New York City that provided a small number of homes with light. Today people all over the world use electric lights.

*Noted inventor Thomas Alva Edison*

**13**

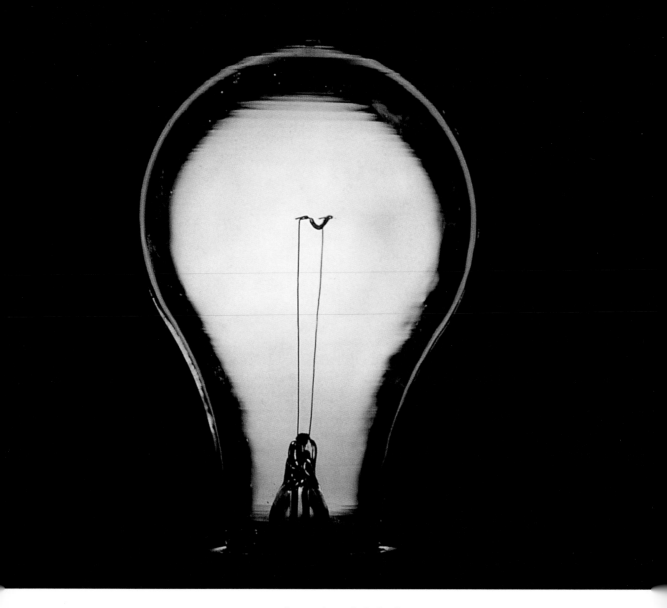

*A modern lightbulb*

*The light from a lighthouse helps guide ships.*

# *LASERS*

All light is made of **photons**, small bits of energy. In a **laser**, these photons work together in a special way. They produce a powerful beam of light that is very sharply focused.

Lasers are in many familiar devices. They are in CD and DVD players. Doctors use lasers to perform some surgery. For example, they use laser surgery on the eyes to help people see better.

*A laser beam slices through an orange.*

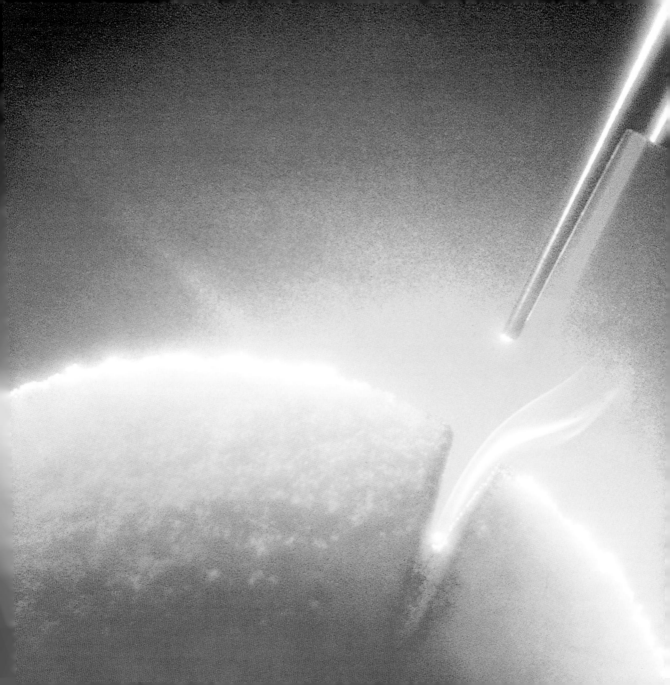

# REFLECTED LIGHT

The sun, as we have seen, is a **source** of light. Lightning and electric lights are other sources.

The moon seems to be a source of light. But it does not have light of its own. It is bright only because the sun shines on it. Sunlight hits the moon and bounces back toward the earth. The moon **reflects** light toward the earth. Most of the things we see do not make their own light. They reflect light.

*The moon reflects the sun's light to Earth.*

## COLOR AND LIGHT

Sunlight looks white, or yellow, to our eyes. What our eyes cannot see is that sunlight is really a mixture of colors.

A red flower soaks up all the colors of the sunlight that strikes it. Only the red color is reflected. In the same way, green leaves soak up all colors except green.

*A red flower reflects the color red.*

# HOW EYES SEE LIGHT

How do we see light? Light enters an opening in the eye known as the **pupil**. Other parts of the eye react to the light. They send messages to the brain. The brain then puts together a picture of what the eye sees.

A person would not be able to see anything without light. An owl has excellent eyesight, even when the light is dim. But even an owl cannot see in complete darkness.

Some people are blind and cannot see anything. Others have limited vision. Some of the causes of vision problems are in the eye. Others are in the brain itself.

*The pupil is the black center of the eye.*

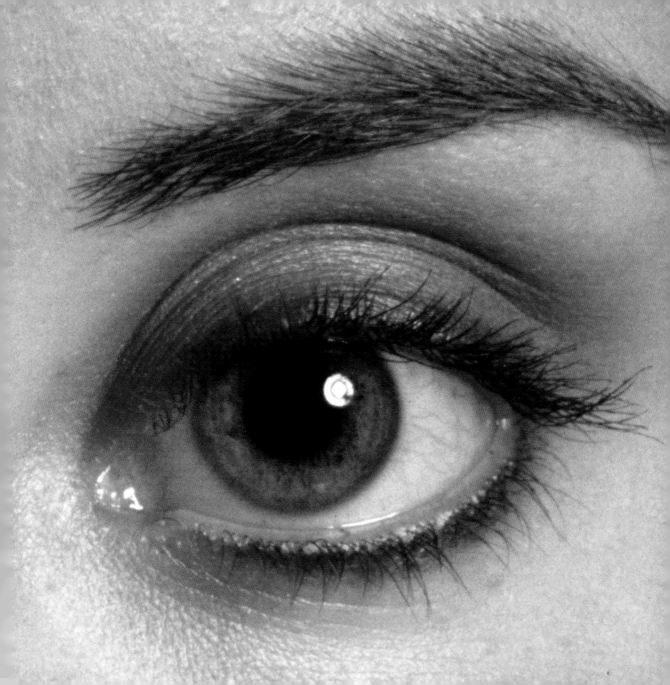

## THE SPEED OF LIGHT

Light travels at 186,000 miles (300,000 kilometers) per second. Sunlight reflected from the moon takes less than one second to reach the earth.

You can block the path of light. You can bend light as well. For example, curved glass bends light. This changes how things look. They can look bigger and closer. Or they can look farther away.

Today, most scientists believe that nothing moves faster than light.

## GLOSSARY

**energy** (EN er jee) — power; the ability to do work

**laser** (LAY zur) — a focused beam of light, used in medicine and communication, among other fields

**photons** (FOH tahnz) — small pieces of light energy

**pupil** (PEW pull) — the part of the eye that allows light to enter it

**reflects** (ree FLEKTZ) — bounces back

**source** (SORSS) — the place from which something comes

## Index

## Further Reading

Branley, Franklin M. *Day Light, Night Light: Where Light Comes from*. New York: HarperCollins, 1998.
Madgwick, Wendy. *Light and Dark*. Austin: Raintree Steck-Vaughn, 1998.
Tocci, Salvatore. *Experiments with Light*. Danbury, CT: Children's Press, 2001. .

## Websites To Visit

www.spie.org/web/oer/august/aug00/maiman.html
www.bell-labs.com/history/laser/
library.thinkquest.org/11924/light.html
www.energyquest.ca.gov/scientists/edison.html

## About The Author

Jason Cooper has written several children's book series about a variety of topics for Rourke Publishing, including *Eye to Eye with Big Cats* and *Money Power*. Cooper travels widely to gather information for his books.